THE WISDOM OF THE SPANISH MYSTICS

THE AUTHOR

Stephen Clissold, O.B.E., was born in 1913 and attended Salisbury Cathedral Choir School. He won an open scholarship to read Modern Languages at Oriel College, Oxford, where he first became interested in the writings of the Spanish mystics. He made his career in the British Council, serving in Denmark, Chile and Turkey, and with the Foreign Office. He is now retired and lives in Bayswater, London. He is the author of many books including Latin America—A Cultural Outline; Latin America—New World, Third World; The Saints of South America; In Search of the Cid; Spain, *and has just completed a longer study of the Spanish mystics. He is married with one daughter.*

THE WISDOM OF THE
SPANISH MYSTICS

SELECTED BY
STEPHEN CLISSOLD

A NEW DIRECTIONS BOOK

Manufactured in the United States of America
First published clothbound and as New Directions Paperbook 442
in 1977 by arrangement with Sheldon Press, London

Library of Congress Cataloging in Publication Data

Main entry under title:

The wisdom of the Spanish mystics.
    (A New Directions Book)
    Bibliography: p. 86
        1. Mysticism—Spain—Collected works.
    2. Mysticism—Catholic Church—Collected works.
    I. Clissold, Stephen.
    BV5072.W5   248'.22'0946   77–7650
    ISBN 0–8112–0663–7
    ISBN 0–8112–0664–5 (pbk.)

New Directions Books are published for James Laughlin
by New Directions Publishing Corporation,
333 Sixth Avenue, New York 10014

TABLE OF CONTENTS

*THE WISDOM OF
THE SPANISH MYSTICS*

★

STORIES AND SAYINGS

THE WISDOM OF
THE SPANISH MYSTICS

SPAIN'S great Catholic mystics flourished in the sixteenth and early seventeenth centuries, when their country was at the height of its military and political power and producing its greatest works of literature and art. The vital élan which led to the discovery and conquest of the New World seemed to have turned inwards too to the mysterious world of the spirit. As a child, St Teresa ran away from home with her small brother to seek martyrdom at the hands of the Moors. When they grew up, he went off with his brothers in search of fame and fortune overseas, while she entered a convent. The brother's adventures are forgotten, but hers remain one of the most enthralling spiritual odysseys of all time.

For nearly seven centuries, Christians had battled against Moslems to win back Spain for the Cross. They had also felt the impact of the more refined culture of their hereditary enemies, and one of the most intriguing questions about the emergence of Catholic mysticism in Spain is whether it owed anything to the teaching of the Moslem mystics, or sufis, who flourished there in the Middle Ages. The greatest predecessor of the Catholic mystics, the Majorcan Ramón Lull, was certainly steeped in Islamic culture and familiar with sufi writings. Striking parallels have also been noted between the austere teaching of St John of the Cross and that of a famous Spanish sufi.

But so far no evidence of any direct links has come to light.

The reconquest of Spain from the Moors bred a fiercely militant, crusading brand of Christianity in Spain which found vent, once the Moslems had all been forcibly converted or expelled, in the persecution of those suspected of Jewish or Protestant leanings. In Northern Europe, the Reformation was beginning to wreck the unity of the Church and to constitute a challenge to Spain, the greatest Catholic power. The Church responded with the Counter-Reformation, of which Spain was a central pillar. This had a repressive side, expressed through the Inquisition, the censorship of books, insistence on strict doctrinal orthodoxy and the tightening up of ecclesiastical institutions. But it was also itself an expression of spiritual fervour and renewal, fed by the same sources which had led to the Reformation. The Spanish mystics reflect this side of the Counter-Reformation—a movement of pure and intense inner spirituality, but operating within the traditional framework of Catholic dogma and institutions. Though the thought might have surprised and even scandalized them—for they shared the prejudices of their age against the Protestant reformers—they speak to men and women of the most varied races and beliefs. Their message is universal and timeless. For it is nothing other than the quintessential affirmation of the Christian faith.

In what do the Spanish mystics differ from their contemporaries who were also pious, and often fanatical Catholics? In the quality as well as the intensity of their spiritual life. The mystic lives for God and directs his life towards the attainment of sanctity, the state pleasing to God. Sanctity is to goodness what genius is to talent. In cultivating the basic Christian virtues and the practices of prayer and religious observance, a soul may suddenly reach a state of spiritual 'take-off'; or rather, a qualitative change supervenes in which the soul itself plays little or no part, but receives an infusion of supernatural grace raising it to the level of 'infused contemplation' in which it experiences what it believes to be a direct awareness of God. Thus the mystic can also be described as one who is in love with God. For the essence of this God with whom he has been granted contact is love, and the touch kindles in the soul an answering flame of love for God and for all God's creatures. The mystic thus appears as a God-intoxicated man. Lull was proud to be called the Fool of Love. The Franciscan reformer St Peter of Alcántara walked through the fields singing aloud the praises of God, so that he was thought to be crazy; St Teresa commented approvingly: 'May God grant us all such holy madness!' St John of the Cross, a poetic as well as a religious genius, composed sublime and passionate love poetry addressed to God.

This fire of love with which the mystic is consumed is no empty figure of speech. It induces or predisposes his soul to receive experiences of a sometimes startling supernatural, or at least paranormal, character. He may pass from the prayerful passivity of recollection, when the mind 're-collects' or gathers together its faculties

5

in a humble waiting upon God, into the trance-like states of ecstasy or onrushing rapture. Inner voices ('locutions') may imprint themselves on the mind, admonishing or exhorting, with unmistakable clarity. He may be granted visions, ranging in type from the 'imaginary' (not in the sense that they are fictitious, but as presented in vivid pictorial form to the imagination) to the 'intellectual' (the awareness of some abstract truth) and these have been subtly distinguished and described by St Teresa and others. He may be lifted bodily from the ground, in the alarming but well-attested phenomenon of 'levitation'. Such things often accompany the intense interior life of the mystic. He does not seek them for their own sake, but rather avoids them and minimizes their significance, realizing that they are less likely to be marks of sanctity than invitations to spiritual pride, sensationalism or self-deception. The writings of the Spanish mystics are full of warnings on this score, and of sound advice on the 'discernment of spirits'—how to distinguish between true and false mysticism, between experiences which promote and those which hinder the authentic spiritual life.

By 1500, when Spain was entering on its path to imperial greatness, the flower of mysticism was in bud. Granada, the last Moorish kingdom on Spanish soil, had fallen. Columbus had discovered America and founded the first settlements. The Inquisition had been established to enforce orthodoxy at home, and the Jews had been either converted or expelled. Although there seems to have been no question of any interaction of Jewish on Catholic mysticism, the high percentage of Spanish mystics with Jewish blood in their veins remains a remarkable fact. St John of Avila, the great missionary, educationalist and spiritual reformer of southern Spain, was of Jewish stock, as were many of his disciples. The prudent St Ignatius was alarmed at the prospect of too many of these 'new Christians' being absorbed into his Society of Jesus, then in its first flush of apostolic ardour and sympathetic to contemplatives. Recent research has shown that even St Teresa, hitherto regarded as the embodiment of pure Castilian Catholicism, was in fact of partly Jewish origin, and her grandfather is known to have been in trouble with the Inquisition.

For this and other reasons—notably the rising ferment in Germany which put such trends elsewhere under suspicion of 'Lutheranism'—new manifestations of personal piety stressing the importance of contemplative prayer and the direct action of God's grace on the individual soul were regarded with misgiving by the authorities. The groups of laymen and women who held such beliefs did not openly challenge the authority and traditional observances of the Church; they seemed rather to be quietly side-stepping them. They did not reject the use of the sacraments, but seemed unwilling to allot them a central place in their religious life. To the vocal prayers prescribed by the Church they preferred to meditate in silence and await the divine illumination. For this reason they came to be known as *alumbrados* or 'the enlightened'. In the 1520s the Inquisition set about savagely suppressing such groups as actual or potential 'Lutherans'. It would be truer perhaps to regard them as potential or low-grade mystics. For the next century and a half, none of the great Catholic mystics of Spain, however impeccable their orthodoxy and way of life, could be sure of escaping denunciation as *alumbrados*. The taint lasted until the late seventeenth century, by which time the splendour of Spanish mysticism had faded.

The dominant influence during the formative stage of Spanish mysticism was that of the Franciscans. The Friars Minor, with their cult of apostolic love and poverty, had always responded to popular aspirations and new currents of spirituality. The writings of one of their friars, Francisco de Osuna, did much to create an interest in the new techniques of contemplative prayer. Although he had links with the *alumbrados*, with whom some of his fellow friars openly identified themselves, he kept on the right side of the line which the Church drew between sound and unsound practices. His books influenced St Teresa and became acceptable, if not always advisable, reading for the faithful. The Franciscan Order was fortunate in having enjoyed the prestige of Cardinal Cisneros (sometimes known in English as Ximenez) who was taken from his monastery to become Queen Isabella's confessor, the reformer of his and other Orders, and later Regent of Spain. The forceful Cisneros combined the asceticism and zeal of the medieval crusader with the humanism of the new age. He encouraged learning and founded the University of Alcalá, from whose presses issued, amongst many other works, those of Master Ramón Lull. The Cardinal took a deep interest in mysticism but seems to have been credulous with regard to pious women (*beatas*) who claimed to be favoured with sometimes dubious revelations. One of the most controversial of these was a woman known as the Beata of Piedrahita, the small town near Avila which became the centre of her cult. The *beata* claimed to be in constant ecstatic touch with Christ, his Mother, and the Apostles, with whom she would hold lengthy conversations for all to hear. Some, like the Cardinal, took her for a saint; others for a deluded eccentric.

The foremost defender of Catholic orthodoxy was the Dominican Order, which had originally been set up to combat heresy in the south of France. Torquemada, the famous Grand Inquisitor, was buried in St Teresa's home town of Avila, and his dread institution continued to be manned chiefly by friars of the same Order. The Dominicans remained intensely suspicious of all manifestations of mysticism, yet they did produce one very popular and prolific mystical writer—Friar Luis de Granada, one of the great masters of Spanish prose. His rich pages, however, lack the note of intimate personal experience which is the hallmark of great mystical writers and this may be one of the reasons why he escaped the persecution which befell others.

As a young man, Friar Luis came under the influence of St John of Avila, a remarkable man whose name is little known to English readers, though he has recently

9

been canonized. In his life-time he was certainly handicapped by virtue of his Jewish origin and by remaining a simple priest rather than accept high ecclesiastic office or join a powerful Order. St John of Avila originally intended to go as a missionary to the New World, but while travelling through southern Spain he was struck by the appalling spiritual abandonment and economic misery of the peasantry, many of whom were only nominal converts from Islam. So Andalusia became the field for his apostolate, and there soon gathered round him a growing nucleus of preachers, evangelists and teachers. St John of Avila combined an intense mystical life with a keen sense of social justice. Soon he was denounced to the Inquisition, mainly, it seems, on account of his denunciations of the callousness of the wealthy. He was eventually released and resumed his apostolate with renewed fervour, working specially to improve the quality of the priesthood through the founding of schools, seminars and colleges. St John was much sought after, by rich and by poor, as a spiritual adviser, and became famous for his 'discernment of spirits'. As the vogue for mysticism spread, attracting charlatans, impostors and deluded hysterics as well as the sincerely devout, this was a most necessary skill. The Beata of Piedrahita was now forgotten, and Spain was agog with the revelations, prophecies and miracles associated with a Franciscan abbess from Cordova, Magdalena de la Cruz. But alas, the abbess fell mortally ill and revealed on her deathbed that a whole lifetime of sanctity and mystical graces had been feigned. They

10

had, she declared, all been the work of a demon called Balban, who had possessed her since the age of five. The repentant abbess was exorcized, recovered her health, and spent the rest of her days in penance; but the scandal remained.

Whilst the Apostle of Andalusia was labouring in southern Spain, the Society of Jesus was beginning to make its influence felt. Its founder was St Ignatius Loyola, a soldier of noble Basque parentage who had been converted through a vision while recovering from a leg wound. Although remaining a man of order, discipline and impeccable orthodoxy, St Ignatius also had many varied mystical experiences. And although he can in a sense be numbered amongst the Spanish mystics, he profoundly distrusted mysticism. He saw that the mystical cast of mind is ultimately subversive of authority. The famous *Spiritual Exercises* which he devised constitute a training manual, in which certain subjects and methods of systematic meditation are laid down in order to achieve a specific frame of mind and certain qualities regarded as desirable for the active life to which the Jesuits were called. The penitent is bidden to advance so far along the path of inner enlightenment, but no further.

The Society of Jesus, particularly in its early years, attracted men whose spirituality was not always at ease within the framework of disciplined meditation devised by the founder. The third General of the Society, St Francis Borgia, himself experienced difficulties. As the Duke of Gandia, he lived piously on his estates whilst winding up his family and official

11

affairs before being free to enter the Society. Amongst the friars and other enthusiasts gathered round his ancestral seat were (St Ignatius warned from Rome) some who 'have been misguided, deluded and misled, following now the right path, now straying from it'. They might even be *alumbrados*; even if they were not, these mystical zealots were not fit company for the Duke, who had to purge his entourage. St Teresa, in the perplexity of her early mystical experiences turned to the future Jesuit saint for counsel and found that 'he was very advanced in prayer, and that he received great favours from God'. It was not until the Jesuits started a college in Avila that she found spiritual directors who could give her the guidance required for the full flowering of her extraordinary mystical vocation. But the Jesuit father who understood her best and who himself became a mystic of a high order, incurred the disfavour of his superiors, who were frankly hostile to any methods of contemplative prayer outside the guidelines of the *Spiritual Exercises*.

By the close of the sixteenth century, the Jesuits' distrust of mysticism had grown so great that the most richly gifted of them was only allowed to remain within the Society on sufferance and to occupy the most obscure and menial of posts. Not that St Alonso Rodríguez was gifted intellectually; he had failed in his modest family business and was told that he would never make the grade as a priest. He was, however, accepted as a lay brother, 'so that he might become a saint'. Whether intended sarcastically or not, the remark proved prophetic. Almost all St Alonso's subsequent life was spent as the door-keeper of a Jesuit College in Palma de Mallorca. He invested this humble and monotonous calling with the drama of high spiritual adventure, hurrying to open the door to each visitor 'as if to his God'. St Alonso's visions and other mystical experiences, which his deep humility and sense of worthlessness led him to distrust, are recorded in the 'Accounts of Conscience' which he wrote regularly for his confessor. His simplicity, the literalness with which he obeyed the orders of his superiors and perhaps the envy aroused by the remark-able effects often caused in novices and visitors who were allowed a few words with him, seem to have exposed him to a good deal of harsh treatment. No one has written more movingly on the sacrificial nature of Christian suffering. Once, when ten Jesuit fathers were on the point of setting sail, Alonso was ordered to prophesy how the voyage would turn out. He replied that it would be a golden voyage. The ship was intercepted by corsairs and all on board made captive. Alonso was publicly reprimanded for failing to warn against the disaster, forbidden to write any more, and even threatened with being brought to trial. It does not seem to have occurred to his brethren that the saint's scale of values was quite contrary to their own, and that for him no voyage was more prosperous or 'golden' than one which ended with a martyr's crown.

Spanish mysticism flourished most vigorously, though not exclusively, in the quiet of the cloister. There in contrast to the world outside where war and

13

exploration, the business of church and state, scholarship, literature and the arts were all male preserves, women might achieve excellence on the same footing as men. They could scale the mystic heights no less heroically than their brothers or fathers. Some, indeed, proved admirably fitted for this role of spiritual conquistadores. But despite the work of men like Cisneros, many convents as well as the monasteries for men still stood in need of reform. During the Middle Ages the social function of the convent often overshadowed the purely religious. To take the veil was the honourable alternative to marriage, specially where dowries were insufficient. The endless wars between Moors and Christians, and among the Christians themselves, drained Spanish manpower and led to a surplus of women. Later, the conquest and colonization of the New World caused a further depletion of the male population. Some women entered a convent as the result of a youthful lapse. Others sought it as a retreat after a worldly life. Widows were frequent recruits; nor was it unusual for married people to separate in order to become monks and nuns. Monastic foundations were expected to house respectable ladies in retirement and disreputable folk in disgrace, and also often to offer hospitality to travellers and visitors. Small wonder, then, that, with this influx of inmates without any true religious vocation, conventual life grew 'relaxed'; the originally austere Rule under which the nuns lived was disregarded or officially mitigated and abuses flourished.

It is not then by chance that we find the most

representative and attractive figure in Spanish mysticism following the vocation of reformer and foundress. Teresa de Cepeda y Ahumada, known to her contemporaries as Mother Teresa de Jesús and to posterity as St Teresa of Avila, took the veil in 1537. For the next twenty years she lived a life which differed little from that of her fellow-nuns in the large, easy-going Carmelite convent of the Incarnation. When she was forty, she underwent a 'second conversion' and began to experience all manner of disturbing phenomena; 'interior voices' and visions of differing types and intensity which she later analysed with incomparable vividness and subtlety in the famous *Life* which she wrote (reluctantly) at the behest of a puzzled confessor. These unprecedented experiences, and the accompanying ecstasies which began to cause a stir in the convent, filled her with terror. She feared that she was becoming a victim of hallucinations or of diabolical possession, and she prayed earnestly to be delivered from them. But by degrees it became clear that these revelations had a purpose; the sanctification of her own spiritual life and a call to help others to achieve the same perfection through a return to strict observance of the Carmelite Rule.

The Carmelite Order prided itself on its antiquity, and claimed descent from the hermits who had settled on Mount Carmel in unbroken tradition from Elijah and the sons of the prophets. It received its formal rule of solitude, total abstinence from meat and uncompromising poverty at the beginning of the twelfth century and migrated into Europe after the

15

failure of the Crusades. A relaxation of these original austerities had been authorized by the Pope in 1432, and it was under this mitigated rule that the Carmelite sisters, who had been a part of the Order since the fifteenth century, now lived. The Incarnation was not a wealthy convent, but the nuns lived a comfortable life some of them attended by their personal servants. They showed no wish to be reformed, and Teresa realized that she would have to begin a new, strictly enclosed foundation, whose dedicated example might in time leaven the whole dull lump of conventional piety. At first this made her very unpopular. 'The nuns', she recalled, 'said it was an insult to them and that I could serve God just as well where I was, for there were others there better than myself, that I had no love for the house, and that it would be better for me to raise funds for it than for somewhere else. Some said that I should be clapped into the prison cell; others—but very few—took my side.'

In the teeth of much opposition and the misgivings of some well-wishers—for she insisted that the new foundation should be without endowments and depend for its maintenance solely on God's providence and the charity of the faithful—Teresa secured a modest house and founded St Joseph's, the first of her reformed Carmelite convents. In this venture she had the support of St Peter of Alcántara, founder of the Discalced or Barefoot Franciscans and himself a mystic. When St Teresa came to know him, he was an old man, so gnarled and withered by a lifetime of austerities that he seemed to be 'made out of the roots of trees'. She adds that after he died she continued to see him in her visions and to receive advice and encouragement from him.

The Father General of the Carmelites came to visit Avila and was edified to see in Teresa's little community 'a picture, albeit imperfect, of our Order as it had been in the early days'. He decided to back the reform and gave her permission to found more convents; more important still, he pledged his support for the foundation of similar houses for friars. The reform spread rapidly, even amongst existing Carmelite convents, including the Incarnation, where Teresa was now called back as Prioress. For the rest of her life, Teresa was constantly on the move and often sick. She encountered hostility too and a new General put a temporary ban on her work, while an unsympathetic nuncio branded her as 'a restless, gad-about, defiant and disobedient woman', founding a new convent here, revisiting her nuns there, winning over vacillating prelates by her tact and persistence, coping with a thousand practical problems of unsuitable accommodation, lack of money or dubious vocations. Nor did her impeccable orthodoxy and transparent goodness prevent the account she had written of her life from being denounced by a spiteful enemy to the Inquisition. St Teresa's reaction was characteristic—she burst out laughing. Even the stern inquisitors finally recognized her book for what it was—the vividly candid and fascinating autobiography of a remarkable woman and a classic of the spiritual life. She also somehow found the time to write other books: an account of her foundations; a simple *Way of Perfection* for her nuns; a profound but lucid analysis of the successive stages of the mystical life, to say nothing of a vast number of letters to correspondents in every walk of life. Many of these have survived and reveal her many-sided personality; foundress and organizer, a woman of unusual warmth, humour and charm, a religious genius who combined humble sanctity with the most exalted mystical experiences which she recorded with the skill of a born writer. In her later years, the disturbing phenomena of trances, visions, interior voices and levitation grew less and less frequent, as she had prayed they might, and left a strength and serenity which sustained her to the end in her unceasing activities as a foundress. One of her contemporaries rightly described her as 'a very great woman in the affairs of this world; and in those of the next, greater still.'

One of the earliest collaborators of St Teresa, and her equal in spiritual stature, was St John of the Cross, the most profound of the Spanish mystics and, in the opinion of some, his country's finest poet. Such was the austerity of his life and his commitment to the cause of reform that his unregenerate brother-friars actually kidnapped him in Avila and kept him imprisoned in a Toledo monastery. Steadfastly refusing to make any compromise and reduced to the extremities of physical exhaustion, he finally made a dramatic escape and sought asylum in a convent of Discalced Carmelite nuns. This searing physical and psychological ordeal acted as a catalyst for his marvellously beautiful and

18

anguished poetry, which comes as near as human language can to conveying the agonies and ecstasies of the mystical experience. In the gloom of his prison cell, he composed the greater part of his luminous masterpiece, *Songs of the Soul and the Bridegroom*, generally called the *Spiritual Canticle*, as well as a number of shorter poems. The *Spiritual Canticle* and the *Dark Night*, another wonderful poem, shorter but movingly evocative both of his bodily escape and the soul's quest for the Beloved, correspond broadly to the first two stages—'purgation' and 'illumination'—in the mystic way. A third great poem, the *Living Flame of Love*, burns with the incandescent serenity of the culminating mystery of the union of the soul with God himself.

St John's other writings consist of elaborate prose commentaries in which with penetrating and subtle analysis the poet seeks to explore the meaning of his verses and of the mystical experience which inspired them. It was in a sense an enterprise foredoomed to failure, for, as he admitted himself, 'human science is not capable of understanding nor experience of describing it; only he who has passed through it will know what it means, though he will find no words for it'. It is in fact the lyrical outburst itself which comes nearest to penetrating the mystery. Nevertheless, in striving to extract the last drop of meaning for himself and for others from the revelations vouchsafed to him, St John of the Cross does succeed in conveying the essence of his teaching: the Way of Negation. We should bear in mind, as the saint

19

himself makes clear, that he was writing primarily for contemplatives, rather than for those who follow the common paths of the Christian life and the precepts of almost unbearable austerity and renunciation are not for beginners but for those well advanced along the path to spiritual perfection.

The Way of Negation involves discarding and stripping oneself bare of everything; a purging not only of the natural appetites but of the human affections and attachments which may be normal and good in themselves but which clutter the void which the contemplative should leave for God alone to fill. He is then plunged into what St John calls the Dark Night: first, the Night of the Senses, which purges the soul of its lower elements and fits it for the spiritual life; then into the still more awesome Night of the Soul, which brings with it the feeling of utter dereliction which all the great mystics seem at some time to have experienced. Temporal props have already been discarded that the soul might be free to receive the divine presence. Then this presence itself seems to be withdrawn. The soul finds it impossible to pray, to dwell on holy things. Yet it can still go on loving through all the desolation and abandonment until, having learned that it knows nothing, understands nothing, can do nothing and wishes nothing for itself, God chooses to reveal himself through the darkness.

St John's austere teaching on the Way of Negation was in strong contrast to the vogue for the dubious and spectacular aspects of mysticism which continued in the ascendant. A new star had now appeared in the mystic firmament—the prioress of a convent in Lisbon who was reputed to perform all manner of miracles and to be blessed with the stigmata, the mere sight of which had been known to convert the most obdurate Moors. St John of the Cross had surprised his brother friars by declining to have anything to do with her, although the nun's blessing had been sought for the standards of the Invincible Armada. The Inquisition had investigated her alleged powers and virtues but found nothing to censure. This was not really surprising, since one of the examiners was the now octogenarian and almost blind friar Luis de Granada, who was so impressed with the nun that he wrote a book about her saintly life and revelations. But the defeat of the Armada and rumours that the prioress was in league with Portuguese national factions conspiring against the Spaniards caused King Philip to order a fresh investigation. This time, a more vigorous application of soap and water was enough to wash away the alleged stigmata and the other tricks by which the nun of Lisbon had built up her reputation as a holy worker of wonders were quickly detected.

By the end of the sixteenth century Luis de Granada, St Teresa, St John of the Cross and Friar Luis de León, another mystic and gifted poet, were dead. A vast literature on contemplative prayer and devotional practices indicated the continuing vigour of the mystical impulse, particularly of its more eccentric manifestations. Some accounts—such as the auto-biography of María Vela, another Avila nun, who seems to have received authentic mystical graces although she clearly suffered from psychosomatic disorders—have had to await publication until our own day. Others, once famous, such as the former best-seller, *The Mystical City of God* which went into a hundred editions in different European languages, are now forgotten. This claimed to be nothing less than the inside story of the life of the Virgin Mary, as revealed and dictated to the prioress of a convent at Agreda. King Philip IV was an avid reader of the book and for more than twenty years kept up a confidential correspondence with its author, who seems to have been a virtuous and intelligent nun who undoubtedly experienced some mystical favours, even if not to the extravagant extent alleged by her devotees.

As the tide of mysticism ebbed in Spain, the two currents of which it had been broadly composed became more clearly differentiated: the external phenomena of revelations, visions, and paranormal occurrences, and the still, small voice in which God conducts his secret dialogue with the human soul. The externals might breed charlatanry, superstition, hysteria and excesses of all kinds; but the hidden practices could undermine the authority of the Church itself. If God spoke direct to the soul what need had the mystic of the mediation of the Church, its liturgy, sacraments and ritual or the intercession of the saints? That was why the Inquisition had persecuted the *alumbrados* and now, in the latter half of the seventeenth century, turned on those who practised a form of passive contemplation known as 'Quietism'. To trace the rise and suppression of this movement first in Italy, and then in France, would take us far from the Spanish mystics. But it was a Spanish priest, Miguel de Molinos, who, finding his native soil unfavourable for propagating the new teaching, moved to Italy where he became its chief prophet. Molinos claimed to draw his inspiration from the fathers of the Church and his great Spanish predecessors, St Teresa and St John of the Cross. His little book, the *Spiritual Guide*, enjoyed immense and sudden success outside Spain, but was at once denounced in that country by the Inquisition and only in recent times has its republication been allowed. Banned by Rome, the *Spiritual Guide* found a welcome amongst the Quakers, who recognized in its teaching a spirit akin to their own.

The passages which follow reflect the many-faceted experiences of a group of mystics within a given historical and cultural-religious context. Though they range from simple nuns or the humble door-keeper St Alonso Rodríguez to learned theologians like Fray Luis de León and St John of the Cross, and reveal many differences of temperament and emphasis, they fall broadly within the same pattern and together form a remarkable chapter of Catholic mysticism. Most of the quotations have been taken from autobiographical writings—diaries, accounts of conscience, memoranda —written at the behest of spiritual directors without any thought of publication. Though many of the greatest mystics, such as St Teresa and St Ignatius were also greatly occupied with practical affairs, and were all fired with loving concern for their fellows, we see them here in the secret intimacy of their spiritual life relating their experiences with unvarnished, and often anguished, honesty, struggling to find words for what is ultimately beyond human power to describe. Yet their message, in its essentials, is clear enough. It offers no short cut to ultimate truth, nor a recipe for instant enlightenment or spiritual bliss. The mystic sees sanctity as a mountain which has to be climbed. The way is that of self-knowledge, self-denial; the divesting of all earthly attachments, until will and desires are totally absorbed in God. 'There must be no more than God and you in the world, for he alone must be all things to you.'

STORIES AND SAYINGS

*silence
contemplation*

I

MASTER RAMÓN LULL taught that a soul in meditation was like a lover sitting alone in the shade of a tree. When passers-by asked him why he was there all on his own, the lover replied: I am alone, now that I have seen and heard you; until then, I was in the company of my beloved.

II

MASTER RAMÓN LULL compared love to an ocean, its waves troubled by the winds and without port or shore. The lover perished in this ocean and with him perished his torments and the work of his fulfilment began.

III

MASTER RAMÓN bade men listen to the lover's call: O Ye that love, if ye will have fire, come light your lanterns at my heart; if water, come to my eyes from which tears flow in streams; if thoughts of love, come gather them from my meditations.

IV

THE MASTER described the lover's path as beset by sighs and tears and lit by love. But when the lover stumbled and fell amongst the thorns they seemed to him as flowers and as a bed of love.

* V *

MASTER RAMÓN declared that when at last they met, the beloved said to the lover: Thou needest not speak to me. Sign to me only with thine eyes, for they are words to my heart, that I may give whatever thou ask of me.

* VI *

MASTER RAMÓN pictured the lover standing before his earthly judges who asked the lover:

Whence art thou? He answered: From love.
To whom dost thou belong? I belong to love.
Who gave thee birth? Love.
Where wast thou born? In love.
On what wast thou nourished? On love.
How dost thou live? By love.
What is thy name? Love.
Whence comest thou? From love.
Whither goest thou? To love.
Where dost thou live? In love.
Hast thou anything but love? Yes, he answered, I have faults and sins committed against my beloved.
Wilt thou find pardon from thy beloved? Yes, answered the lover, I have found in my beloved mercy and justice and thus I dwell between fear and hope.

26

VII

MASTER RAMÓN described how the judges tried to make the lover recant and taunted him with being the Fool of love:

Say, O Fool, what is love? Master Ramón answered: Love is that which casts the free into bondage, and gives liberty to those that are in bonds. And who can say whether love is nearer to liberty or to bondage? The judges asked: Say, thou that for love's sake goest as a fool! For how long wilt thou be a slave, and forced to weep and suffer trials and griefs? He answered: Till my beloved shall separate body and soul in me. Say, Fool of love! If thy beloved no longer cared for thee what wouldst thou do? I should love him still, he replied. Else must I die; seeing that to cease to love is death and love is life. The lover saw himself taken and bound, wounded and killed, for love of his beloved. And his torturers taunted him: Where is thy beloved? He answered: See him here in the increase of my love and the strength it gives me to bear my torments.

★ VIII ★

ST JOHN OF THE CROSS gave the following advice: In the evening they will examine you in love. Learn to love as God wishes to be loved and cease to be what you were.

★ IX ★

ST JOHN OF THE CROSS warned: Love does not consist in feeling great things, but in nakedness and suffering for the beloved. Love as if there were only God and yourself in this world so that your heart may not be held back by anything human.

* X *

FRIAR LUIS DE LEÓN, for all his great learning, taught: Love is only found, understood and won by love.

* XI *

ST ALONSO the Door-keeper wrote of himself: I pay no attention to the life of my body but only to the life of my soul. All the rest I regard as nothing compared with pleasing my God, for God is my life and my whole good. There is nothing more to be sought.

* XII *

ST ALONSO was sitting in the refectory one supper-time lost in meditation. The Superior sent him word to get on with his meal and eat up his plate. His companions were surprised to see him take up his spoon and begin scraping away vigorously with it. When they asked him what he was doing the saint, who always obeyed orders literally, replied that he was trying to do as he had been told—eat up his plate. Alonso only desisted when they explained that the Superior had really meant him to eat the food on his plate—not the plate itself. St Alonso on hearing the door-bell would raise up his heart to God and exclaim: Lord, I shall open the door for you, for love of you! As he hurried to answer it he would feel as glad as if it really was God he was going to let in, and he would say: I'm coming, Lord! When someone rang loudly and impatiently his natural reaction was to get upset but he mastered this feeling and by the time he had reached the door he had calmed down and he opened it as if the caller had given only a gentle ring. No matter who the caller might be, it seemed to him that he was opening the door to his God.

✴ XIII ✴

ST ALONSO described prayer as follows: A petition to God and the Virgin for four loves: first, the love of God; secondly, the love of Jesus Christ Our Lord; thirdly, the love of the Virgin Our Lady; fourthly, the love of men for each other until the end of the world and for all men who are in the world and who will be in it until it ends.

✴ XIV ✴

ONCE, when St Alonso was engaged in earnestly praying that he might be granted joy in suffering and love his persecutors, he had the following experience: Suddenly, before he realized what was happening, there came upon him a sort of fiery comet, like those which fall from heaven at night. It came down on him from on high and wounded him in the side so that it left his heart on fire with love for his neighbour. And it seemed to him that he could not wish ill towards his neighbour, even if he were to do the most terrible things to him.

＊XV＊

ST TERESA used to remind her nuns: It is not a matter of thinking much, but of loving much. So do whatever most kindles love in you.

＊XVI＊

AMONGST THE PAPERS found after St Teresa's death were these maxims: Love makes labour light. Love alone gives value to all things.

＊XVII＊

MARÍA VELA, a sufferer from sudden bouts of lockjaw and other psychosomatic disorders, told her confessor: I was given to understand that the Lord wished me to be the martyr of love, and that none other than the divine love itself would be my executioner. I was left filled with a longing to die at the hands of life itself.

＊XVIII＊

MARÍA VELA's confessor disapproved of her practice of going without food or drink for a long time after receiving Communion. The nun was strengthened by an interior voice which assured her: Today you shall

30

have no need of earthly nourishment. I know that Lord, she humbly replied. But please tell my confessor, he is the one who needs convincing.

✶ XIX ✶

ST TERESA, recognizing a spiritual giant in the tiny figure of St John of the Cross, wrote to a friend: Though he is small in stature, I deem him great in the eyes of God.

✶ XX ✶

A NUN once asked St John of the Cross whether he composed his verses when he was in a state of ecstasy. Sometimes God gave them to me, he replied, and at others I sought them out for myself.

✶ XXI ✶

A NUN who was asked to give evidence at St John's beatification declared: Our holy Father John of the Cross was for some years the friend and confessor of Ana de Jesús [a saintly prioress] who told me that on a number of occasions God allowed one of them to know what was passing in prayer with the other and when they later saw and told each other, this proved to be true. Another nun cited an instance of this: Once, when on a journey by night, St John fell over a cliff, he felt as if he were stopped in mid-air and so was able to seize hold of some bushes and climb back to the path. At the same hour, Mother Ana was at her prayers when she had a sudden vision that Friar John was in great danger and she commended him most earnestly to God. A few days later, St John visited her and she asked him how his journey had been and whether he had found himself in some danger or trouble. Why do you say that? he asked, and she told him what had passed when she was at prayer, and the exact day and hour. Then it was you who stopped me, he said, and related what had happened. The nun added that Mother Ana de Jesús had told her this herself.

* XXII *

In REPLY to those who asked whether a soul could make progress without the guidance of a spiritual master, St John of the Cross declared: The soul which has virtue but remains on its own without a master is like a burning coal which is left to itself; it loses its glow and grows cold.

* XXIII *

St JOHN OF THE CROSS taught: Do not imagine that, because someone seems not to excel in the virtues you think he should have, he is not precious in God's sight on account of things you have not thought of.

* XXIV *

A CERTAIN FRIAR once acquired a fine new habit of which he was excessively proud. The others, mindful of their strict rule of poverty and humility, took him to task. The friar retorted that a shabby habit did not make a man holy, and that he had once seen a tunic said to have been worn by our Lord which was made of the finest stuff. St John of the Cross, who was Prior at the time, overheard this remark and replied sternly: Whether the tunic belonged to our Lord or not, he had no need of coarse habits, since he was perfect. But we, who are sinners and need to mortify the flesh, do need them. And he made the friar take off his new habit there and then and put on an old one.

* XXV *

ST JOHN OF THE CROSS taught: All creatures are crumbs dropped from God's table. And he who subsists only on them goes hungry like a dog, since the scraps they feed on never satisfy their hunger but only stimulate the appetite.

* XXVI *

ST JOHN OF THE CROSS, bitterly persecuted by his brother friars, wrote: If you would come to possess Christ, never seek him without the cross. Those who pass for the friends of Jesus Christ know little of him, for we see them going in search of solace rather than of his bitter sufferings. God values your readiness to face suffering and deprivation for love of him more than all the consolations, spiritual visions and meditations which you may have.

✶ XXVII ✶

WHEN ST TERESA learned that St John had been imprisoned, she commented: It is terrible what treatment God allows his friends to suffer. But then we should not really complain, for that is how he treated his own Son.

✶ XXVIII ✶

DESPITE the great affection and respect which St Teresa and St John of the Cross felt for each other, the young friar did not hesitate sometimes to reprove the foundress: When you make your confessions, Mother, he told her, You think up the prettiest excuses for your sins!

✶ XXIX ✶

ONE DAY St John of the Cross confided to a friend that there was still something which prevented his complete detachment from earthly affections. Fetching a bundle of papers he threw them into the fire and watched them burn. They were the letters he had received from St Teresa and treasured dearly.

✶ XXX ✶

ST ALONSO wrote: Union, attained by the grace of God with the help of prayer in time of tribulation and trial, grows in the soul through sufferings. If it overcomes sufferings it grows more perfect; if it does not overcome them, the opposite is true. So we have to set more store by affliction than by consolation, by opposition than by approval, and so things are better when they seem worse. That is to say, when we have opposition to overcome for God, we have the chance of gaining greater sanctity and perfection. Sanctity is not to be measured by favours and consolations, but by suffering greatly for God.

* XXXI *

LUIS DE LEÓN, returning to his university after five years' imprisonment by the Inquisition, resumed his lectures with the words: As we were saying yesterday.

* XXXII *

FRAY LUIS, who loved to escape to the peace of the countryside, wrote: Christ dwells in the fields. St Teresa, busy in the convent kitchen, used to say: The Lord walks amongst the pots and pans.

* XXXIII *

ST PETER CLAVER, inspired by St Alonso to dedicate his life to the Negro slaves, wrote: In order to follow Jesus Christ in the love of souls, we must persecute ourselves; in order to be his we must cease to belong to ourselves; we must accept what is bitter as if it were sweet. Of all the adversities which fall upon us for his sake, there is no higher path in life, nor anything more pleasing to God, than to suffer willingly for Christ.

35

⋆ XXXIV ⋆

St Peter used to ask God to teach him the patient obedience of a donkey: Every time I do not behave like a donkey it is the worse for me. How does a donkey behave? If it is slandered, it keeps silent; if it is not fed, it keeps silent; if it is forgotten, it keeps silent; it never complains, however much it is beaten or ill-used, because it has a donkey's patience. That is how the servant of God must behave. I stand before you, Lord, like a donkey.

⋆ XXXV ⋆

One day St Peter saw a Spaniard jostle a black slave-girl who was walking through a narrow street with a basket of eggs on her head. The basket fell to the ground and the slave burst into tears as she feared the anger of her mistress. Peter began to console her and bid her have faith. He then righted the basket with his stick and stooped to gather up the eggs. The slave-girl found that not one of them had broken.

⋆ XXXVI ⋆

A Negro who attended St Peter in his last illness noticed one night a light coming from the sick man's cell. Opening the door he found the bed empty and the saint suspended several feet above the ground absorbed in prayer. When the ecstasy was over, the Negro helped the sick man back into bed. Peter made him promise not to breathe a word of what he had seen until after his death.

⋆ XXXVII ⋆

St Toribio, Archbishop of Lima, was so charitable to
the poor that he not only gave them the food from
his own table, but sometimes the silver dishes on
which it was served. This worried his sister who was
in charge of the household and she would then send
off a servant to buy back the dishes. One day, when
he was out visiting, the archbishop was approached by
a distraught mother who begged him to provide a
dowry for her daughter so that she could marry.
St Toribio carried no money on him but he dis-
mounted and gave the woman his mule, saying: Take
this and sell it; but quickly, before my sister sees!

⋆ XXXVIIII ⋆

St Mariana of Quito was favoured with visions and
other mystical graces which she divulged to no one
except her confessor. The latter, thinking to test her
obedience and to edify the girl, ordered her to give a
full account of them to her young niece. St Mariana
was greatly distressed, but did as she was told. The
niece, amazed at what she heard, hurried away to
write it all down. But on reaching her room she found
herself unable to recall a single word. In great confu-
sion she returned to her aunt and asked her to repeat
everything she had said. Tell my confessor, Mariana
replied with a smile, that I have done what he ordered.
But it seems that our Lord wants us to keep these
secrets to ourselves.

37

MARÍA VELA, watching the stone-carvers at work, observed: Carving the image of a saint out of a block of stone calls for great care and skill. How many blows the stone has to be struck before the eyes and other features begin to emerge, and what labour it costs the craftsman! If the stone could only feel, how it would cry out and resist. The same happens on the spiritual level. To raise up children to Abraham out of stone, whatever is not needed has to be chipped away with hammer blows of mortification in order to lay bare the eyes, humble, simple and chaste, of a saint, and all those other features which make up his serene and modest bearing. And for this, we need to be like stone, leaving ourselves in the hands of the craftsman without complaining, though he hacks us to pieces; for if we turn away and try to ward off the blows the heavenly likeness will never be made manifest.

MARÍA VELA compared suffering to the mark by which God's slaves are branded: In the eyes of the world it appears to be the sign of a slave or a fool to embrace the cross and to forsake pleasure, honours and possessions; yet in the eyes of God there is no wiser choice.

ONCE MARÍA VELA had a vision of Christ seated on a majestic throne. When I desired to embrace my Lord in that glory, she told her confessor, I found myself embracing the crucified Christ. It was thereby signified to me that in this life we should seek only the Lord despised and suffering on the cross; we shall enjoy that other Lord of glory in the life to come.

★ XLII ★

St Teresa exhorted her daughters: Detach your heart from all things; seek God, and you will find him.

★ XLIII ★

St John taught: Strive always to bend yourself to the following:

not to what is easiest, but to what is most difficult;

not to what is most pleasing to the taste, but what is most bitter;

not to what you find most pleasurable, but most disagreeable;

not to what is most restful, but most laborious;

not to consolation, but to what leaves you disconsolate;

not to the more, but to the less;

not to what is highest and most precious, but to what is lowest and most worthless;

not to something you want, but to want nothing at all;

not to go seeking the best of temporal things, but the worst;

and in all there is in the world, to bear nakedness, emptiness and poverty for Jesus Christ.

39

St John expressed his teaching in the following paradoxes:

If you would come to taste all things; then do not seek to taste anything.

If you would come to possess all things; then do not seek to possess anything.

If you would come to be everything; then do not seek to be anything.

If you would know everything; then do not seek to know anything.

To reach that for which you have no taste, you have to go where you have no taste to go.

To reach what you do not know, you have to go where you do not know.

To come to possess what you do not possess, you have to go where you have no possessions.

To reach what you are not, you have to go where you are nothing.

When you dwell on any one thing, you cease to cast yourself upon the All.

To pass from all things to the All, you have to deny yourself wholly in all things.

And when you come to have the All, you must have it without asking for anything.

For if you wish to have anything at all, then you do not have your treasure purely in God.

* XLV *

María Vela, overwhelmed with a sense of her own nothingness and deep in ecstatic prayer, seemed to hear Christ speak these comforting words: This nothingness which you see yourself to be is what I love in you. From this nothingness you will ascend to the heights.

★ XLVI ★

St Teresa, when young, venerated a pious old woman whom she once asked: Do you not long to die, Mother? I do; I am so eager to see my Bridegroom! Not at all, my daughter, the old woman replied. I want to live as long as I can, so that I may go on suffering for him. This won't be possible after my death; there will be plenty of time to enjoy being with him then.

★ XLVII ★

St Teresa used to say: I like hearing the clock strike. It means that this life has become shorter by one hour and that I'm one hour nearer to seeing my God.

★ XLVIII ★

St Teresa told her nuns: We shall never succeed in knowing ourselves, unless we seek to know God. By looking at his greatness, we become aware of our own vileness; by looking on his purity, we see our own impurity; by considering his humility, we see how far we are from being humble.

★ XLIX ★

María Vela wrote: The Lord often wishes to visit the soul but finds it so occupied with temporal things that he does not do so.

St Teresa, who practised strict obedience to her confessors even when her mystical experiences went far beyond their comprehension, explained how she was saved from any conflict of loyalties: Whenever the Lord commanded me in prayer to do one thing, and the confessor commanded me to do something else, the Lord would then speak to me again and tell me to obey my confessor, and would then change the latter's mind and make him countermand the orders he had given me.

* LI *

Writing of the mystic's difficulty in knowing whether his experiences were divinely inspired or not, St Teresa declared that, so long as he received them with true humility, they can do no harm, even were they to come from the Devil; whereas, if humility is absent, they can do no good, even if they come from God.

* LII *

St Alonso wrote: When the love of God enters the soul it shows up all our faults as a sunbeam shows up every particle of dirt. The same light which reveals the splendour of God reveals our own vileness.

* LIII *

St Alonso wrote: How can the soul enjoy the contemplation of God? Only by understanding that

42

it can know nothing of him. The more ignorant it realizes itself to be, the sweeter it finds him. Even when the soul enjoys him, it cannot understand him, for he can be understood only by himself. When the soul has stripped away all comprehensible things, it is left with God the Incomprehensible.

★ LIV ★

FRAY LUIS DE LEÓN wrote: Christ himself implants love in those that love him. He passes into their hearts and dwells in their souls. Christ looks out from their eyes, speaks with their tongues, works through their senses. Their faces, their movements are Christ's, who occupies them wholly. So intimately does he take possession of them that, though his nature in no way destroys or corrupts their own, there will be nothing seen in them at the last day, nor will any nature be found in them, other than his nature.

★ LV ★

ST TERESA advised those who were practising contemplative prayer: Do not fret about what you cannot understand, nor rack your brains trying to fathom it. Many things are not for women—nor, for that matter, for men either.

★ LVI ★

ONE DAY St Ignatius went to pray in a church outside Manresa. The road led along a river-bank. When he sat down to rest, his eyes fixed on the running water and his mind in prayer, he experienced an intense and sudden enlightenment. Althought he could never find words to describe what had been revealed to him there, he used to say that all things seemed to have been made new, and that what he understood in that moment exceeded everything that he had learned during his whole life.

✶ LVII ✶

SISTER MARÍA DE AGREDA was questioned by the Inquisitors who suspected that she might be an impostor or a heretic. Did she claim, they asked her, to have actually set eyes on God himself in her visions? Miserable creature that I am, she replied, how could I, the most wretched sinner alive, dare to behold God in this my mortal state? But God does sometimes grant awareness of himself through a veil or mental image. This grace seems to have been given me. Not the divine presence itself; not face to face with him, as we long to be. That privilege is only for the blessed.

✶ LVIII ✶

ST JOHN OF GOD used to go through the streets of Granada and collect the sick and destitute people he found there. The Archbishop sent for him and told him that he ought to send away the good-for-nothings who were giving his hospital a bad name. The saint, who had once led a roving life himself, answered respectfully: My Lord, I know of only one man in my hospital who answers to that description, and that is the sinner John of God

★ LIX ★

SOME MOORS, who were sitting round a fountain, taunted St John of God about his faith and poured scorn on his belief in miracles. John, who was a very burly fellow, answered: Is it not miracle enough that God constrains me not to throw you into the water?

miracle

★ LX ★

ST JOHN OF GOD was advised by his friends to go to a city where the King was holding court, in order to beg alms for his hospital. He did so and many people gave generously. But after a few months he left empty-handed. I found even more folk there in need of help, he explained. Charity is to be practised wherever you are.

generosity

★ LXI ★

PEDRO VELASCO was in jail on a charge of murdering a man in a quarrel, whilst Anton Martin, the dead man's brother, vowed he would move heaven and earth to have the murderer brought to the gallows. In the meantime, Anton made plenty of money as a pimp and led a dissipated life. But he also gave liberally to John of God, who never ceased praying for his conversion. Coming face-to-face with him one day, John pulled out a crucifix and cried: Your brother's blood calls 'Vengeance', but God's blood, which he shed for your sins, calls 'Mercy'! If you would have God forgive you first forgive your enemy! Anton, seized with contrition, was reconciled with Pedro Velasco and had him released from prison. The two men spent the rest of their lives working with John in his hospital, Velasco taking the name of Peter the Sinner and Anton Martin becoming John's administrator and successor.

⋆ LXII ⋆

A POOR widow, whose son was away at the wars, used to set aside each day part of her scanty food for John of God's hospital. Once she had nothing to spare but a few pinches of salt. Soon afterwards her son returned and told her that he had been discharged and had had to beg his way home almost starving. One day, he added, he received no more than a few pinches of salt to keep him alive. Struck by the coincidence, the widow asked what other alms he had been given. As it had amounted to so little, he remembered very clearly and described to his mother just what food, and how much of it, people had given him. She found to her amazement that it corresponded in form and quantity to what she herself had saved at the same time for John of God.

46

JOHN OF GOD's confessor, the prudent St John of Avila, grew alarmed when he heard that his convert was going about Granada not only rescuing the sick in the streets but taking fallen women back to his hospital. He wrote urging him to be cautious: You must not let your zeal for doing good blind you to the danger you may be running yourself. There is nothing gained if you try to drag others out of the mire only to fall into it yourself. So I beg you once more to set time aside for prayer and for hearing mass each day, and a sermon on Sundays. Beware of getting involved with women, for you know that the Devil may use them to ensnare God's servants. Don't be taken in by those who say: We only want to help them. If you don't take care, good intentions can be dangerous. God does not want us to do good to others at the cost of doing harm to our own souls.

THE COUNT OF FERIA had a great admiration for St John of Avila who, besides being a man of deep spirituality, was much esteemed for his wise advice on all practical matters. If I were asked who would make a good Pope, the count used to declare, I would answer: Master Avila! Or a good judge? Master Avila! Or a good captain? Master Avila! Or a good king?: Why, Master Avila!

THE DOMINICAN Melchor Cano, like some other theologians, disapproved of the mystics and accused them of wanting to turn everyone into contemplatives. If a cobbler mends his shoes the worse for doing his spiritual exercises, he wrote, or a cook spoils his broth, it is no excuse to say that it was because they were at their prayers and devotions. I have always held that the test of a man's religion is whether he performs his office the better for it.

religion: test of prayer + action

★ LXVI ★

ONE EVENING St John of God called to beg for alms at the house of a wealthy Marquis who was playing cards with his friends. The gamblers good-humouredly clubbed together and handed him twenty-five ducats. When his back was turned, they began to argue whether he was a saint or a fraud. I'll soon settle the issue! the Marquis declared, and they laid their bets. Disguising himself in some old clothes, he then hurried after John, who failed to recognize him but listened with compassion to the practical joker's tale of woe. When he had finished, John at once offered him all the money he had on him—the twenty-five ducats. The Marquis rejoined his friends and throwing the coins on the table exclaimed: Those who have backed him for a saint—though he's a simpleton, too—have won! The next day he went to the hospital and handed John not only the twenty-five ducats, but all the money he and his friends had been ready to gamble away.

love of the poor

48

LXVII

ONCE, finding the body of a beggar who had died in the street, John of God asked a rich man if he would have the charity to give him Christian burial. I have no money to throw away on dead bodies, the man exclaimed indignantly. This poor man is as much your brother as he is mine, John replied, and as you have the means, whereas I have not, I leave it to your conscience to discharge this duty. Then he strode out of the house, leaving the corpse on its threshold. The servants were too superstitious to touch it, and the authorities were known to be dilatory. In great alarm the rich man sent a messenger to beg John to come back and promised to pay him the cost of twenty shrouds if only he would take the body away.

LXVIII

ST JOHN OF THE CROSS taught: Contemplation is nothing other than the peaceful and loving infusion of God which, if accepted, inflames the soul with the spirit of love.

LXIX

J UIS DE GRANADA wrote: Prayer is the issuing of the soul to receive God, when he comes in his abundant grace and the soul draws him to itself. Prayer is the standing of the soul in the presence of God, and of God in the presence of the soul.

FRIAR JUAN FALCONI described what came to be called the Prayer of Simple Regard: To walk with our gaze fixed simply on God. To contemplate Christ is to look on him simply with the eyes of faith, without asking oneself or imagining anything further, but just to go on looking at him, believing in him and loving him.

There are no rules or methods. We must simply place ourselves in the presence of God and remain there, resigning ourselves into his hands to do with us whatever he will. We shall soon find that there is little we need to do or to understand, and little cause to fear being led astray.

SISTER ANA MARÍA, Prioress of a Franciscan convent, would find herself transported into ecstasy while she was preparing to receive the sacrament of Holy Communion. She wrote: I felt the presence of my God beside me, and He said: Embrace me! Tomorrow you are to receive me, and will you not now embrace me? As he said this, I felt myself caught up in God's embrace and filled with majesty, grandeur and union with him, and such great blessings that it seemed to me that there was nothing further to be desired on earth. This union lasted many days and brought with it a great suspension of powers and a loving gratitude which permeated all my senses. To be caught up in God's embrace and to be made aware of his presence was something perceived inwardly, not with the eyes

of the body. With it there came an inner understanding, though my senses were fully conscious of it
too. And once I had entered into this state, I lost the
very memory of how I had reached it and any wish to
leave it again.

<h3 style="text-align:center">*LXXII*</h3>

St Alonso told his confessor: It has sometimes
happened that, before going to bed, I have begun
praying and continued to do so while at the same time
I was really fast asleep. And when I fall asleep as I am
praying, I pray in exactly the same way in my sleep
as I do when I am awake. I sleep, but my heart keeps
watch.

<h3 style="text-align:center">*LXXIII*</h3>

St Alonso gave this description of how he entered
into contemplation: After praying, Lord, let me know
you, let me know myself, I would find myself raised
up above all created things, as if transported to another
region. There, alone in the divine presence, is commu-
nicated to me a knowledge of myself and of God
through the clear light of heaven rather than through
any process of reasoning. I am snatched out of myself
and placed in the infinite being of God.

<h3 style="text-align:center">*LXXIV*</h3>

St alonso wrote: Hardly did I begin to raise my
heart to God when, in a moment, I used to find
myself in the divine presence, before saying anything

or speaking at all of love. I was wounded by love
merely through looking at God. The more I tried to
flee, the greater was the presence which God com-
municated to me even as I fled. I struggled, and let
myself be beaten by God. Then suddenly there came
upon me a sort of ray or lightning flash which
wounded my heart, and this wound was the will of
God.

⋆ LXXV ⋆

ST ALONSO gave this advice to the novices: Look for
God in all things, and you will find him and always
have him at your side. Look for God in all men, and
serve them as images of him.

⋆ LXXVI ⋆

MARÍA VELA, who regarded herself as one of the
thieves crucified with Christ, wrote: I stood for a
quarter of an hour with outstretched arms beside the
cross, and told the Lord that there was another thief
craving his mercy. I had stolen what belonged to
him—my own body and soul—and delivered them
up to evil. Now I desired to commit another theft, of
far greater value to myself, by stealing from him his
will. I was given to understand that, by loving him, I
should attain my desire in accordance with the words:
I love them that love me. As I yearned for a single
spark of this divine fire I was made aware that in the
heart of Christ our Lord is fire enough to set the whole
world aflame, and that I should seek it there.

ST TERESA, describing the experience of rapture, wrote: It seems that the soul no longer animates the body, which thus loses its natural heat and gradually grows cold, though with a feeling of very great sweetness and delight. Rapture is generally irresistible. Before you can be warned by a thought or do anything to help yourself it sweeps upon you so swiftly and strongly that you see and feel yourself being caught up in this cloud and borne aloft as on the wings of a mighty eagle. You see and know that you are being borne aloft, yet know not whither. For though this brings delight, the weakness of our nature at first makes us afraid. We need more courage and strength of mind than in the earlier stages of prayer, to risk everything, come what may, and leave ourselves in God's hands to be borne away wherever he will. In such extremity I have often wanted to resist and striven against it with all my might for fear of being deluded, especially when this happens in public, but often when I am alone also. At times, by great efforts, I have had some success; but it has been like struggling against a great giant and it has left me utterly exhausted. Sometimes it proved quite impossible, and my soul and usually my head too have been carried away. At times my whole body has been lifted from the ground. This has happened only rarely. Once, when we were together in the choir and I was kneeling down to communicate. This greatly distressed me as it seemed most extraordinary and bound to attract much public attention.

I ordered the nuns (for it occurred after I had been elected prioress) to say nothing about it. At other times, when I began to see that the Lord was going to do the same with me (once when some ladies and persons of rank were there and we were listening to a sermon on our patron's feast) I lay down on the ground and they came round to hold me down, but it was noticed all the same.

∗ LXXVIII ∗

A FRIEND once complimented St Teresa on being of illustrious ancestry, which was much prized in her day. It is enough for me, Father, that I am a daughter of the Catholic Church, she answered, and to have committed one venial sin would cause me more distress than to be descended from the lowliest and meanest folk in the world.

∗ LXXIX ∗

ST TERESA and another nun were spending a night in an empty house which was to be turned into a convent. The nun, thoroughly scared, got it into her head that she was going to die in the night and she asked the foundress what she would then do all alone in such a place. I will think about that if it should happen, St Teresa calmly replied. But in the meantime, Sister, let us go to sleep!

∗ LXXX ∗

A CERTAIN contemplative used to spend part of every night in ecstasy. During one of these raptures it was revealed to him that a friend, whom everyone accounted a good Catholic and a patriotic Spaniard, was secretly preparing to defect to Africa and become a Moslem. The contemplative at once sent a message imploring him not to give way to such a wicked temptation. If a servant of God can read another's thoughts like that, the man said to himself in amazement, how much more must God himself see into the secrets of the heart and punish the evil he finds there! So he repented and ended his days in true devotion.

* LXXXI *

ST TERESA wrote of ecstasy: It is like being in the throes of death, except that the suffering brings with it such joy that I cannot think of any proper comparison. It is martyrdom, harsh yet sweet. For whatever earthly things are offered to it, sweet though the soul may normally find them, it now seems to reject them. It is fully aware that it longs only for its God; not for any particular attribute of his, but for God in his wholeness, although it has no knowledge of what it so ardently desires. This is nowadays the habitual state of my soul. Whenever it is not distracted by something else, it is plunged into these death-yearnings. And when it feels their onset, it is seized with fear because it cannot die. But once they come upon me, I would have them last for the rest of my life. Yet the pain is so intense as to be almost unendurable. The sisters, who have grown accustomed to seeing me in this state and so understand it better, tell me that sometimes my pulse almost ceases to beat. My bones are all disjointed and my hands are sometimes so stiff that I cannot clasp them together. These pains in my wrists and throughout my body can last for more than a day and make me feel my bones are still out of joint. Oh what torment it is for a soul in this state to have to return to the company of men, to see and watch the sorry farce of this life of ours and to waste time in satisfying such bodily needs as eating and sleeping!

★ LXXXII ★

A PRIEST to whom St Ignatius dictated his spiritual memoirs recorded an experience which befell the saint not long after his conversion: When he was in hospital it often happened that he saw, in broad daylight, something hovering in the air close beside him and he found much pleasure and solace in gazing at it because of its exceeding beauty. He could not easily make out what this apparition was, but it seemed to have something of the serpent about it and to be all aglitter with what appeared, although it was not so, to be eyes. He took great delight in beholding this thing and the more he gazed upon it, the greater consolation he found, and he was grieved when it disappeared . . .

Later, after being restored to health, he knelt down beside a nearby cross to give thanks to God. Thereupon there appeared to him the apparition which he had seen many times and never discovered what it was—the beautiful thing which, as I have said, seemed to be aglitter with many eyes. But kneeling there before the cross, he now saw that the colour was not so lovely as it had seemed before and it was clearly revealed to him that it was the devil. So whenever it appeared again, which it did frequently for a long time, he used to drive it off with the stick he carried.

＊LXXXIII＊

ONE DAY, St Teresa recalled: I was in a chapel when the devil appeared on my left side, looking most horrible. I noticed his mouth in particular, which was fearful to behold, since he was speaking to me. A great flame seemed to be issuing from his body, bright and translucent. He said to me, in terrible tones, that although I had escaped from his clutches he would get me again. I was stricken with terror and crossed myself as best I could, whereupon he disappeared but was soon back again. This happened to me twice. I did not know what to do. There was some holy water nearby, so I threw it in his direction and he vanished for good.

＊LXXXIV＊

ST TERESA, describing how she dealt with subordinate devils, wrote: I took a cross in my hand and God truly seemed to give me strength, for in a short time I found myself a different person and had no fear of taking them on, for it seemed to me that I could easily rout them with that cross. Come on now, all of you! I cried. I should like to see what you can do to me, for I am a servant of the Lord! They seemed indeed to take fright at me for I grew quite calm and bold, so that to this day I have lost all my previous fear of them. Although I sometimes see them I have hardly ever been afraid of them since and in fact it is they who seem afraid of me. The Lord of all things has given me such power over them that I take no more notice of them than of flies.

⋆ LXXXV ⋆

ONE of St Teresa's maxims was: Cultivate holy boldness, for God helps the strong.

⋆ LXXXVI ⋆

ONE DAY when St Teresa was praying, it seemed to her, without knowing how or why, that she had been plunged straight into hell. She later understood that in this way the Lord wished to show her the place prepared for her in recompense for her sins. This happened in a mere moment. Yet though I might live many years, she recalls, it seems impossible for me ever to forget it. I seemed to be on the threshold of a long, narrow passage, like a very low, dark and cramped oven, the bottom of which seemed to be covered with slimy, foul-smelling water full of evil reptiles. At the far end was a cavity scooped out of the wall like a cupboard where I found myself closely confined. But all this was a sight pleasing to the eyes compared to my feelings in that place. What I am saying is no exaggeration. Indeed, it would be quite impossible to exaggerate or even fully to grasp all that I am trying to say. I felt a fire within my soul which quite defies my power to describe. I have endured the severest pains in the course of my life, the worst the doctors tell me, which it is possible to suffer, amongst them the contraction of my nerves when I was paralysed, and many other torments, including some caused by the devil, and still live. Yet none of these could bear comparison with the agony I felt at that time, especially since I knew it would be everlasting.

All such things, then, are nothing in comparison with the soul's agony. It feels itself so weighed down and suffocated, in such deep and hopeless affliction, that I can find no words to express it. To say that the soul is being continuously torn from the body fails to describe its torment, for death at least might hold promise of an end, but here it is the soul itself which is being torn apart. The fact is that it is quite beyond my power to describe that fire within the soul, that despair, which is greater than the severest torments or pains. I could not see my torturer, but I felt as if I were being burnt and torn to pieces and, I repeat, that the fire and despair within me were the worst of all. In that pestilential place, deprived of all hope of solace, it was impossible to sit or lie down, for there was no room to do so. I had been squeezed into what seemed a hole in the wall, and the very walls, which were hideous to behold, kept pressing in upon me and stifling me. There was no light there; only the blackest darkness. Yet I do not know how it could be so, for though there was no light, whatever could terrify the eyes was still clearly seen . . .

All this happened nearly six years ago, yet even as I write about it my blood runs cold with terror. I can recall no time of trial or torment endured here below which does not seem trifling in comparison with this; it makes me think that generally we have no real reason to complain. And so I repeat that this experience was one of the greatest mercies that the Lord has bestowed on me, for it has been of great benefit to me in making me lose the fear of any tribulations and contradictions I may suffer in this life, and in giving me strength to endure them and to thank the Lord for delivering me, as I now believe, from those other terrible and endless torments.

∗ LXXXVII ∗

St Teresa was once driven back to her convent in a carriage belonging to a great lady she had been visiting. A friar who was an enemy of the reform began abusing her as she got out: So you're the 'saint' who is taking everybody in—and going about in a carriage too! The nuns were scandalized, but St Teresa listened to him meekly and remarked: He is the only one with the courage to tell me my faults! But from that day no one could persuade her to travel in anything but the poorest and most uncomfortable of carts.

∗ LXXXVIII ∗

St Teresa wrote of the Franciscan reformer St Peter of Alcántara: For forty years he never had more than one hour and a half's sleep between nightfall and

morning, and such sleep as he had he took sitting
down or on his knees, for his cell was only four
and a half feet long. He always went barefoot and
wore sackcloth next to the skin, and usually ate once
in three days. Once he spent three years in a monastery
where he knew his brother friars only by their voices,
for he never raised his eyes from the ground. For
many years he never set eyes on a woman, but
when he became old he said it was all the same to
him, whether he looked at them or not. When at
prayer he would commonly be transported into
ecstasy as I myself witnessed. Yet for all his holiness I
found him a delight to talk to, since he had a lively
intelligence and was very courteous. Though he died
soon after I had come to know him, St Peter appeared
to me frequently in visions and continued to give me
encouragement and counsel. Once he reprimanded
me sharply when I seemed tempted to abandon the
principle of absolute poverty on which my conventual
reforms were based.

★ LXXXIX ★

SOMEONE who did not know St Teresa well was surprised to see her sitting down for once to a good meal.
There's a time for partridge and a time for penance,
the saint is said to have remarked.

★ XC ★

ST PETER, though experiencing many mystical
phenomena himself, warned: Do not seek revelations,

marvels or extraordinary things, but rather those things which our Lord teaches in his Gospel and which Holy Church declares unto you. The devil often transforms himself into an angel of light in these strange things. Set your affections on your cell and on recollection. Commune within yourself with God. Offer your heart naked to his Majesty and place yourself in his hands. Give yourself to prayer and heavenly matters and observe obedience. When you are beset by the noise and turmoil of the world, plunge deep into divine contemplation . . . as if, in all creation, there were no other things save God and your own soul.

★ XCI ★

ST ALONSO, referring to his supernatural experiences, declared: So great is my aversion to such things that I would prefer not to speak or write about them and that no one should know of them. For they bring more danger than profit and the world esteems them highly, though there is little light in them, when it should make much of solid virtues. Sanctity consists in the love of God and of one's neighbour, and in profound humility, patience, obedience and resignation, and the imitation of Christ our Lord. In this there is no danger; but in the other there is.

★ XCII ★

ST TERESA used to say: Be gentle with others, but stern towards yourself.

⋆XCIII⋆

St John of God used to go through the streets with his collectingbox and call out merrily: Do yourselves a good turn, my brothers, do yourselves a good turn! People were curious to learn what he meant. John explained that he was not begging favours from them, but just giving them the chance to store up a little treasure for themselves in heaven.

⋆XCIV⋆

Master Ramón taught: When you hear men speak great things, or listen to the singing of the minstrels, or the sound of the wind in the trees, or of the waves breaking on the shore—then love God all the more because of it.

⋆XCV⋆

Not long after its foundation by St Teresa, the convent of St Joseph's was infested by a plague of lice. St Teresa led the nuns in procession from cell to cell, singing penitential psalms and some verses she had composed for the occasion and sprinkling holy water on the straw mattresses. The lice disappeared and never troubled them again. The nuns regarded their deliverance as a favour specially vouchsafed to the Foundress so that her daughters should not be distracted whilst practising contemplation.

St John of the Cross warned: Anyone who dabbles in meditation and thinks he hears interior voices when in a state of recollection immediately ascribes them to God—Then God answered me!—whereas it is not God at all, but simply they themselves giving the answer they happen to fancy.

★ XCVII ★

Friar Francisco de Osuna, noting the popular vogue for mysticism, complained: There are those who begin crying out that they cannot contain themselves and only in this way can they find relief. Others burst into floods of tears, groan aloud, or fall down as if dead; others tremble and gesticulate. For the most part it is their own spirit which causes all this, often quite innocently, for the heart is greatly agitated by their ardour and good intentions. But the wisest course is to keep quiet and hold back these cries and shouts. Some people make such efforts to master their feelings that they start bleeding at the nose and mouth and suffer great pain.

★ XCVIII ★

Another friar, John of the Angels, gave this warning: God deliver me from ecstatic talk about devout and spiritual matters; from turning up the white of the eyes and fixing them rapturously upon the heavens, from deep and tender sighs, and from exclamations like: O good Jesus! O my Love! Ah, Love of my Life! From all such you should abstain, and from excess of outward humility, and from all that may cause you to be marked out and appear eccentric.

* XCIX *

A DISCIPLE of St John of the Cross gave the following account of an episode which he witnessed: A nun of Avila called Mother Peñuela was much persecuted by the devil, for it often happened that, when she wished to enter the Carmelite convent, the devil caused her to fall down before she reached the doorway, and so heavy did she then become that no matter how many people tried to lift her up they were unable to do so. Two yoke of oxen could not have made her budge from the spot. Then word would be sent to John, who would come out of the monastery to the church where Mother Peñuela had fallen to the ground. And without his uttering a word but simply by standing there, the nun would get to her feet perfectly free of the devil.

* C *

A CERTAIN PRIEST, who had been with St John of the Cross trying to exorcize a nun who was possessed by an evil spirit, related the following story. At first, we had no success. When we broke off to attend divine service the possessed nun, who was sitting with the others in the choir, was suddenly lifted bodily into the

65

air and remained suspended there upside down. The nuns broke off their singing in horror but St John strode forward and commanded: In the name of the Holy Trinity, Father, Son, and Holy Ghost, I order you to return this nun to her place! At these words the possessed woman at once completed her somersault and went quietly back to the stalls. After service the rites of exorcism were resumed and the nun was at last freed from the mischievous spirit.

⋆ CI ⋆

ST JOHN OF THE CROSS once had a vision in which Christ appeared to him and asked him what favour he wished to be granted. Lord, that you may send me trials to suffer for your sake, and that I may be despised and held of no account, he replied. St John died not long afterwards, in disgrace with his Order and in the custody of unfriendly friars.

⋆ CII ⋆

A CERTAIN NUN of Lisbon was famed for her visions, prophecies and other reputed wonders. When St John of the Cross was in that city a brother friar suggested that they should go together to visit the holy woman. God forbid! St John exclaimed. Why should we go to see someone who is taking everybody in? Not long afterwards the nun was discovered to be a complete fraud, and the stigmata on her hands and feet were washed off with water.

St John of the Cross was once accosted in the streets
of Granada by a woman who accused him of being
the father of the baby she was carrying in her arms.
Who, then, is its mother? asked St John. The woman
declared that the mother was of noble birth and lived
in Granada. And where did she live before coming to
Granada? he asked. The woman answered that she
had lived there all her life. And how old is the child?
St John asked. One year old, was the reply. Then
truly he must be the fruit of some great miracle, the
saint remarked, for I have been in this city only a few
days, and he went calmly on his way.

St John of Avila, known as the Apostle of Andalusia
and famous for his skill in the 'discernment of spirits',
proposed some useful yardsticks for testing the
authenticity of mystical experiences and revelations.
First, whether they were in agreement with the
teaching of the scriptures and the Church. Secondly,
whether those who received them were sure that they
were quite free from treachery, since 'the Devil can
slip in a lie between a thousand truths'. Thirdly, did
they help the visionary to lead a more virtuous, truly
Christian life, or simply make him continuously talk
about them? Did the vision leave behind a sense of
serenity or merely excitement and curiosity? Did it
make for deeper humility, with the knowledge that

God should favour unworthy sinners with such things, or encourage the belief that those so favoured must be something special? The answers to such questions should help to show whether the visions and revelations stemmed from God or the devil.

★ CV ★

ONE DAY, when St Teresa was taking her turn in the kitchen, she was carried off into ecstasy still holding a frying-pan in her hand. The nuns were alarmed—not to see her in ecstasy, for they had grown used to that— but because they feared she might spill the cooking oil, which was the last they had in the convent.

★ CVI ★

ONE OF St John of Avila's converts was a young woman of good family called Doña Sancha Carrillo. She was converted after listening to St John preaching, when she seemed to see his words issuing from his mouth like fiery darts. She spent the rest of her short life living as an anchoress in a cell built for her near her parents' house and she was favoured with many intense mystical graces. Luis de Granada, who knew both St John and Doña Sancha, offers two possible explanations for her mortal sickness: One was her distress at seeing the starvation and suffering around her caused by a severe drought, and a craving to offer up her own life in expiation. Another was the fever caught after she had plunged into a tank of cold water

68

in order to subdue the temptations of carnal lust which
were assailing her.

* CVII *

FRIAR LUIS related the following: There was a gentleman of rank in Seville who suspected that his wife was
unfaithful to him and was sorely tempted to kill her.
He went to speak to Master Avila and seek his counsel.
Together they entered a church, and the Master
tried to turn him from his evil designs, but all in vain:
I am much grieved that you are so little moved by the
counsel I gave you, Master Avila said to him, but as
you are still troubled in spirit, I pray you to kneel
down before that image of Our Lady over there and
beseech her to deliver you from the great affliction
you are in. This he did and at once felt a great sense of
relief and reassurance. He hurried to tell the Master, and
they both gave thanks to God for having delivered him
from the doubts which had been tormenting him about
his wife's fidelity.

* CVIII *

A PRIEST, who attended St Ignatius in his old age,
recorded what the saint had once told him of his
conversion: One night, as he lay sleepless in bed, he
saw very clearly a likeness of Our Lady with the holy
child Jesus. After gazing on them for a long time he
felt such a sense of joy and so great a loathing for all
his past life, especially for the things of the flesh, that
it seemed to him that his mind was wiped clean of all
the images of them on which it had been accustomed

to dwell. And from that hour until this, which is August 1553, when these words are being written, he never yielded consent, even in the least degree, to any desires of that kind. And since this was the effect, it can be taken that this thing was of God, though he never dared declare as much, nor do more than affirm that it was as has been said above. But his brother and all others of his household began to perceive from outward signs how great an inner change had taken place in his soul.

⋆ CIX ⋆

St Alonso described a vision granted him when he was ill: One night, as I was lying in the darkened bedroom, our Lord entered it with his blessed Mother. The radiance shining around them was so bright that the light by which the room was normally lit seemed a mere shadow by comparison. They placed themselves before me near the foot of the bed, so that I could easily see them. The Lord was on the right-hand side. Sickness had driven all thought of holy things from my mind but with the light and joy which this visit brought all my pain and suffering suddenly vanished. But the moment the vision faded, these feelings of intense joy in soul and body left me and I became once more a sick man in great pain.

⋆ CX ⋆

St Teresa wrote: Once when I was praying on the feast of the glorious St Peter I saw Christ beside me, or more exactly, I felt him to be at my side, for I saw nothing with the eyes of the body nor with those of the soul. But Christ seemed to be close beside me and I saw that it was he who seemed to be speaking to me. I was utterly ignorant about such visions and was very frightened and at first I could do nothing but weep. But as soon as he spoke to me I regained my usual composure and became calm, happy and free of fear. And it seemed to me that Jesus Christ stayed at my side, but as this was not an imaginary vision I was unable to see in what form; but I clearly felt he was at my right-hand side all the time and that he witnessed everything I was doing.

⋆ CXI ⋆

St Teresa recalled another experience: One day whilst I was at prayer, the Lord was pleased to show me no more than his hands. Their beauty was quite beyond description. I was filled with a great fear, as usually happens when the Lord begins to grant me the experience of some new supernatural favour. A few days later I also saw that divine face, and the sight seemed to transport me quite beyond myself. I could not understand why the Lord was revealing himself to me gradually in this way, for later he was to grant me the favour of seeing him whole. Later I learned that his Majesty was making allowances for the weakness of my nature. May he be for ever blessed, for so vile and base a creature as myself would not have been able to bear it, and it was because he knew this that he acted in this way.

DESCRIBING the radiance of the figures seen in her visions, St Teresa wrote: It is not a dazzling splendour but a soft whiteness and infused radiance which brings great delight to the eyes and never tires them with the sight, nor does its brightness prevent us from gazing upon this divine beauty. It is a light so different from what we know here below that the sun's brightness seems dim by comparison with that brightness and light which is revealed to our gaze and makes us reluctant ever to open our eyes again. It is like looking at very clear water running over a bed of crystal reflecting the sun, as compared with looking at a very muddy stream running over the earth beneath a cloudy sky. It seems to be natural light, whereas the other is artificial. It is light which knows no night and since it remains for ever light nothing can dim it.

ST TERESA wrote of one of her most moving visions: Beside me, on my left, I saw an angel in bodily form. He was not tall but small, and very beautiful. His face shone so brightly that I took him to be one of those angels of the highest rank which seem to be all aflame. He must have been one of those they call Cherubim. In his hands I saw a long golden spear which appeared to be tipped at one end with a fiery point. This he seemed to plunge several times into my heart. It seemed to penetrate to my very entrails and when he pulled it out, I felt as if he were taking them with it, and I was left on fire with a great love of God. So sharp was the pain that I groaned aloud, yet so great was the sweetness of that extreme pain that I could not wish it to end, nor could the soul rest content with anything but God. It is not a physical but a spiritual pain, though the body has a share, indeed a large share, in it. It is so sweet a lovetoken of that love which passes between the soul and God that if anyone thinks I am lying I pray God, in his goodness, to grant him some taste of it.

★ CXIV ★

THE NUNS thought that Sister Ana María de San José was dying. But she was in a state of ecstasy of which she later gave an account: In this ecstasy or death I was carried to judgement. Before that Judge and many of his friends whom he had as witnesses, my whole life was laid bare—every sin, every imperfection, in detail, and every favour and benefit which I had received until then. And the Judge ordered that I should judge myself and pass sentence and so I became my own judge, just as if that soul were not mine. And I gave sentence that it deserved to be accursed of God and unworthy of his presence. But they pardoned me and seemed to confirm me in grace . . . I found myself outside the body, far, far removed from my own self and drawn to God. I was utterly detached from all things, as if nothing else existed for me but God alone. And in this solitude I tasted tranquillity and peace and a serenity of soul beyond comparison.

SISTER ANA MARÍA wrote of another vision: It was given me to know the mystery of the most Holy Trinity and the distinction of the divine persons, and each of them wrought in me great and marvellous things. From that divine being there issued forth splendours which were their attributes—power, wisdom, mercy and other attributes—and I apprehended their work. So immense and distinct were they that no human tongue can describe them, and they moved me to a sense of blessedness, glorification, prostration, annihilation and a most glorious joy that God is what he is and that he was communicating his blessing to me as fully as if I were, in a sense, God myself by nature. Then faith and hope seemed to drop away, for everything became, as it were, the sight and possession of God.

SISTER ANA MARÍA believed that she was sometimes transported in ecstasy to distant lands: Then I feel that our Lord is carrying me off in spirit within himself. At other times I feel he is carrying off my heart, and when he carries off my heart, he first asks me when I have finished communicating: Now I am in Ana's heart; whatever is asked of me I will grant it. Sometimes he says: Now let us go to Japan. I have many friends there labouring for the conversion of souls and we need to visit and strengthen them. I am given to understand an infinite number of things about the errors of the Indians and how mightily God works amongst them dispelling the blindness of those who are in darkness and breathing his spirit into those who labour there. It has often happened to me that I have been borne through the air as if in flight, and sometimes I find myself amongst a crowd of Indians of different nations, with a copy of the Cathechism in my hand, and they on their knees listening to it.

★ CXVII ★

St Rose of Lima believed that her vocation was neither to marry nor to become a nun, but to lead a life of prayer and mortification at home. To discourage the many suitors attracted by her extraordinary beauty, she secretly practised fearful austerities which began to leave their mark on her features. But still people came to see her, attracted now as well by the fame of her virtues. So Rose, embarrassed by this reputation, prayed that her appearance might simply be 'modified'—neither dazzling in its beauty, nor yet so disfigured as to make others suspect her self-inflicted penances.

★ CXVIII ★

A visitor once came to see St Rose in her garden and found herself struggling against a swarm of mosquitoes. Oh, you are killing my friends! Rose exclaimed in distress. We have made a pact together, she explained, I don't disturb them, and they leave me alone. In fact, they join me only to sing God's praises.

Each morning Rose would open the doors and windows and say: Now, my friends, it is time to praise God! The mosquitoes would hum cheerfully round her for a while and then fly out into the garden. In the evening, she would summon them again: Come, my friends, let us praise God before going to rest! The insects would repeat their performance and then fly off for the night.

∗ CXIX ∗

A PIOUS lady, curious to see whether St Rose deserved her reputation, visited her home in expectation of an edifying conversation. She could not conceal her disappointment on finding that Rose refused to be drawn. It is better to talk *with* God rather than *about* him, Rose at length remarked, and withdrew to her room to pray.

∗ CXX ∗

St TERESA taught: The highest perfection does not consist in feelings of spiritual bliss nor in great ecstasies or visions nor yet in the spirit of prophecy, but in bringing your will into conformity with that of God.

∗ CXXI ∗

St ALONSO wrote: The highest perfection consists in this, that all a man's thoughts, words and actions be directed solely to the honour and glory of God. A man ought to work with the supreme desire of making his will conform in every way to the will of God, and of bringing it into such close union with him that he not only rejects evil but even the good which God may not desire. He must not let any adversity, whether spiritual or temporal, disturb his peace of soul, but desire only what God wishes and receive it from his hand.

⋆ CXXII ⋆

St Alonso taught that if God chooses to work through us we should not think that it indicates any merit on our part. With a stick as his instrument God can work wonders; nor is the stick anything other than a stick because of this. That is what God did with Moses' rod.

⋆ CXXIII ⋆

St Teresa gave her nuns the following advice: Let your desire be to see God; your fear, that of losing him; your grief, that you are not enjoying him; your joy, that he may take you thither. Then you will live in great peace.

⋆ CXXIV ⋆

St Teresa taught: Never hear or speak ill of anyone except yourself. And when you find pleasure in this, you may be sure you are making some progress.

⋆ CXXV ⋆

St Teresa also taught: One person, who is perfect in all things and who is moved with the truly ardent love of God, can do more good than the many who are lukewarm.

✴ CXXVI ✴

St Teresa gave her nuns three precepts: First, to love one another; secondly, detachment from all created things; thirdly, true humility. Though I mention this virtue last, she wrote, it is the chief one and includes all the others.

✴ CXXVII ✴

St John of the Cross taught: Whatever goodness there is in us is on loan. It is God's handiwork, and he is the owner of it. God and his handiwork are one.

✴ CXXVIII ✴

St John of the Cross said: The whole world is not worth a man's thought, for that is due to God alone; whenever we turn our thoughts to something other than God we steal what is his.

✴ CXXIX ✴

St John of the Cross gave the following counsel for spiritual perfection: Let yourself be taught, let yourself be commanded; let yourself be placed under subjection and despised; then you may be perfect.

✴ CXXX ✴

St Teresa wrote: Just as there are seasons in the world around us, so there are in our interior life. We cannot expect it to be otherwise.

⋆ CXXXI ⋆

St Teresa used to exhort her nuns: God preserve us, my daughters, when we do something which is less than perfect, from excusing ourselves by saying: We are not angels; we are not saints! Although we are not, it is fine to think that, with God's help, we can be if we make the effort. Provided we do not hold back, have no fear that he will deny us. We came here for no other purpose than to strive, so all hands to the plough, as they say.

⋆ CXXXII ⋆

St Peter Claver kept the precepts given him by St Alonso sewn into his habit. One of them was: There must be no more than God and you in the world, for he alone must be all things to you.

⋆ CXXXIII ⋆

In a letter of spiritual advice to a brother priest St John of Avila wrote: Of that which passes in your own heart between God and yourself you should say nothing, as the married woman says nothing of what passes when she is in bed with her husband.

⋆ CXXXIV ⋆

St Teresa wrote to the prioress of one of her convents: God preserve all my daughters from priding them-selves on knowing Latin! I would rather they took pride in being simple, as is often the way with saints, than in displaying their learning.

⋆ CXXXV ⋆

To a gentleman who had often escorted her on her journeys, St Teresa wrote: May God send us more trials to suffer for his sake—even if they are only fleas, hobgoblins and bad roads!

⋆ CXXXVI ⋆

Seeing one of her prioresses wearing an old thread-bare cloak, St Teresa took it from her saying: Have mine instead. It's new, and more suitable for someone young. I'm an old woman and should wear an old cloak.

⋆ CXXXVII ⋆

St Peter of Alcántara, whose harsh austerities used to amaze those who knew him, would tell them: I have made a pact with my body to allow it no respite in this life so that it may enjoy rest everlasting in the next.

⋆ CXXXVIII ⋆

St Peter of Alcántara exhorted St Teresa to see that the vow of poverty was strictly observed in her convents, but in the right spirit. If we find there are some convents where the nuns suffer real want, he explained, it is because they are poor against their will and cannot help it and not because they are following Christ's precepts. I am not singing the praises of poverty as such but of poverty suffered patiently for the love of Christ, and still more of poverty desired, sought and embraced for his love.

⋆ CXXXIX ⋆

St Peter of Alcántara used to urge his disciples to be like the fishes which, whenever a storm blew up and the waves rose high, would find safety in the still depths of the ocean. So, he would say, when the world around you is full of sound and fury, plunge all the deeper into divine contemplation.

⋆ CXL ⋆

St John of the Cross taught: The purpose of God, who is divine by nature, is to make us gods through participation, as fire transforms all things into fire.

⋆ CXLI ⋆

After St Teresa's death, the following lines were found inscribed in her breviary:

Let nothing perturb you, nothing frighten you.
All things pass;
God does not change.
Patience achieves everything.
Whoever has God lacks nothing.
God alone suffices.

81

St Ignatius summed up the purpose of life in these words: Man is created to praise, reverence and serve our Lord and thereby to save his soul. The other things upon the face of the earth are created for man to help him pursue the end for which he is created. Whence it follows that man has to use them insofar as they help him towards his end and to renounce them insofar as they are a hindrance. For this reason it is necessary that we should become indifferent to all created things in everything that is within the domain of our free will and not forbidden to it. We should for our part not desire health rather than sickness, wealth rather than poverty, a long life rather than a short life, and similarly in everything else, only desiring and choosing that which leads us more surely towards the end for which we have been created.

St Francis Solano, when under the impetus of love, would move like the wind so that no one could keep pace with him. One Christmas, a friar caught sight of him rushing along carrying some gifts under his cloak and called after him: Where are you off to so fast, Friar Francis? To meet my Beloved! came the reply. The friar later discovered that his Beloved was a toothless and bed-ridden old hag—one of the many sick and destitute whom the saint had taken under his care.

⋆ CXLIV ⋆

ST FRANCIS SOLANO decided to teach a covetous friar
a lesson. One day, the friar found him carrying a heavy
box on his shoulders which he referred to mysteriously
as his 'treasure'. The friar eagerly offered to give him
a hand in carrying it. The friar grew more and more
curious, but St Francis would say nothing more until
they reached the church. There he opened the box and
revealed his 'treasure'—the body of a small child to
whom he proceeded to give Christian burial.

⋆ CXLV ⋆

MASTER RAMÓN LULL declared that the Sultan must
have been truly amazed at the Pope and the Christian
princes, because they strove to win back the Holy
Land by the same methods as Muhammad, who used
force of arms, whilst neglecting those of their Lord
Jesus Christ and the Apostles, who converted the world
through preaching and suffering martyrdom.

⋆ CXLVI ⋆

THE ABBOT OF MONTSERRAT taught: A man who thinks
he can reach the height of contemplation without firm
perseverance is like one who sets out to climb a
mountain but turns back before reaching the top; or
who lights a fire of fresh green sticks but angrily puts
it out again because at first it gives out a lot of smoke;
or who reaps the wheat before it ripens; or like a
monkey which starts nibbling a nut but throws it
away before reaching the kernel because the shell

tastes bitter. So without firm perseverance there is no benefit from fire, wheat or nuts—and no perfect contemplation.

ANSWERING those who said it was spiritual pride and presumption to try to practise the higher forms of prayer and to strive after perfection, the Abbot of Montserrat put the following question to them: Suppose a king has a mind to promote one of his kitchen servants to be steward, as he thinks him well fitted for this, but the servant begs to be excused because he likes working in the kitchen and eating the good food there, or because he is lazy, or afraid of taking responsibility—would he not be much to blame? In the same way, a Christian who holds back from the call to follow a more excellent way of life on the plea of humility is guilty of lacking real fervour and conviction.

A WISE PRIORESS noticed that a lay sister, whom she knew had no true vocation for such things, was claiming to see visions, work miracles and to be favoured with frequent raptures. The prioress sent for her and said: Sister, we don't need you here for your raptures, but for washing the dishes. After the lay sister had left the convent, the Inquisition—less merciful than the prioress—pronounced her to be possessed by the devil and threatened her with the stake.

MARÍA DE AGREDA, famous for her ecstasies and mystical writings, was widely believed to have been miraculously transported to America to preach the gospel to the Indians. When questioned as to whether this was true, the nun, who did not quite know herself what to make of her experiences, replied: I have always had doubts about whether it was my actual body that went. I cannot tell in what way I was conveyed there, as I was in a trance at the time. Sometimes I seemed to see the earth beneath me, and the sea in all its wonders. But all this could simply have been revealed to me by God. Once I had the impression that I was distributing rosaries amongst the Indians. I am inclined to think that the angels must have been permitted to assume my bodily form, and that God just let me see what was happening. It is affirmed that the Indians really *did* see me amongst them over there; but I suspect that it may have been an angel impersonating me.

SOURCES OF THE QUOTATIONS

St Alonso Rodríguez
    Autobiography
    Precepts given to St Peter Claver
Ana María de San José
    Autobiography
Bernardino de Laredo
    Ascent of Mount Sion
Francisco de Osuna
    Third Spiritual Alphabet
St Francis Solano
    Quoted in Stephen Clissold, *The Saints of South
    America*
St Ignatius Loyola
    Autobiography
    Spiritual Exercises
St John of the Cross
    Ascent of Mount Carmel
    Sayings of Light and Love
    Commentary on the *Dark Night of the Soul*
    Miscellaneous writings
St John of God
    Quoted in Manuel Gómez Moreno, *San Juan de
    Dios*
    Quoted in Norbert McMahon, *St John of God*
Juan de los Angeles
    Manual of the Perfect Life
St Juan de Avila
    Audi, filia
    Letters

Juan Falconi
  Straight Road to Heaven
Luis de Granada
  Book of Prayer and Meditation
Luis de León
  Commentary on the Song of Songs
  Names of Christ
María de Agreda
  Answer to an Inquisitor, quoted in T. D.
  Kendrick, *Mary of Agreda*
María Vela
  Autobiography
  Book of Mercies
St Mariana of Quito
  Quoted in J. Morán de Butrón, *Vida de Santa Mariana*
Abbot of Montserrat (García de Cisneros)
  Ejercitatorio de la Vida Espiritual
  Extracts from Kathleen Pond, *Spirit of the Spanish Mystics*
St Pedro de Alcántara
  Treatise on Prayer and Meditation
St Pedro Claver
  Quoted in Angel Valtierra,
  Peter Claver, Saint of the Slaves
Ramón Lull
  Book of the Lover and the Beloved
  Life (by anonymous contemporary)
St Rosa of Lima
  Quoted in Pedro Loaysa, *Vida de Santa Rosa de Lima*

St Teresa of Avila
  Life
  Book of Foundations
  Exclamations of the Soul to God
  Letters
  Precepts
  The Mansions
  Meditations on the Song of Songs
  Accounts of Conscience
  Verses
  Way of Perfection
St Toribio de Mogrovejo
  Quoted in Vicente Rodríguez Valencia, *Santo Toribio de Mogrovejo*

New Directions Paperbooks

Complete descriptive catalog available free on request from
New Directions, 333 Sixth Avenue, New York 10014.   † Bilingual